HIV/AIDS
and the world of work

ILO code of practice

HIV/AIDS
and the world of work

International Labour Office   Geneva

Copyright © International Labour Organization 2002
First published 2002

Publications of the International Labour Office enjoy copyright under Protocol 2 of the Universal Copyright Convention. Nevertheless, short excerpts from them may be reproduced without authorization, on condition that the source is indicated. For rights of reproduction or translation, application should be made to the Publications Bureau (Rights and Permissions), International Labour Office, CH-1211 Geneva 22, Switzerland. The International Labour Office welcomes such applications.

Libraries, institutions and other users registered in the United Kingdom with the Copyright Licensing Agency, 90 Tottenham Court Road, London W1T 4LP [Fax: (+44) (0)20 7631 5500; email: cla@cla.co.uk], in the United States with the Copyright Clearance Center, 222 Rosewood Drive, Danvers, MA 01923 [Fax: (+1) (978) 750 4470; email: info@copyright.com] or in other countries with associated Reproduction Rights Organizations, may make photocopies in accordance with the licences issued to them for this purpose.

ILO

HIV/AIDS and the world of work. ILO code of practice. International Labour Office,
ILO Global Programme on HIV/AIDS and the World of Work, Geneva, 2002

Code of practice, AIDS, disabled worker, rights of the disabled, rights, equal employment opportunity, occupational health. 15.04.02

ISBN 92-2-111633-6

Also published in French: *Le VIH/SIDA et le monde du travail. Recueil de directives pratiques du BIT* (ISBN 92-2-211633-X, Geneva, 2002); and in Spanish: *El VIH/SIDA y el mundo del trabajo. Repertorio de recomendaciones prácticas de la OIT* (ISBN 92-2-311633-3, Geneva, 2002).

ILO Cataloguing in Publication Data

The designations employed in ILO publications, which are in conformity with United Nations practice, and the presentation of material therein do not imply the expression of any opinion whatsoever on the part of the International Labour Office concerning the legal status of any country, area or territory or of its authorities, or concerning the delimitation of its frontiers.

The responsibility for opinions expressed in signed articles, studies and other contributions rests solely with their authors, and publication does not constitute an endorsement by the International Labour Office of the opinions expressed in them.

Reference to names of firms and commercial products and processes does not imply their endorsement by the International Labour Office, and any failure to mention a particular firm, commercial product or process is not a sign of disapproval.

ILO publications can be obtained through major booksellers or ILO local offices in many countries, or direct from ILO Publications, International Labour Office, CH-1211 Geneva 22, Switzerland. Catalogues or lists of new publications are available free of charge from the above address, or by email: pubvente@ilo.org
Visit our website: www.ilo.org/publns

Photocomposed by the ILO, Geneva, Switzerland
Printed in France

DTP
NOU

Preface

The HIV/AIDS epidemic is now a global crisis, and constitutes one of the most formidable challenges to development and social progress. In the most affected countries, the epidemic is eroding decades of development gains, undermining economies, threatening security and destabilizing societies. In sub-Saharan Africa, where the epidemic has already had a devastating impact, the crisis has created a state of emergency.

Beyond the suffering it imposes on individuals and their families, the epidemic is profoundly affecting the social and economic fabric of societies. HIV/AIDS is a major threat to the world of work: it is affecting the most productive segment of the labour force and reducing earnings, and it is imposing huge costs on enterprises in all sectors through declining productivity, increasing labour costs and loss of skills and experience. In addition, HIV/AIDS is affecting fundamental rights at work, particularly with respect to discrimination and stigmatization aimed at workers and people living with and affected by HIV/AIDS. The epidemic and its impact strike hardest at vulnerable groups including women and children, thereby increasing existing gender inequalities and exacerbating the problem of child labour.

This is why the ILO is committed to making a strong statement through a code of practice on HIV/AIDS and the world of work. The code will be instrumental in helping to prevent the spread of the epidemic, mitigate its impact on workers and their families and provide social protection to help cope with the disease. It covers key principles, such as the recognition of HIV/AIDS as a workplace issue, non-discrimination in employment, gender equality, screening and confidentiality, social dialogue, prevention and care and support, as the basis for addressing the epidemic in the workplace.

This code is the product of collaboration between the ILO and its tripartite constituents, as well as cooperation with its international partners. It was adopted unanimously by a Meeting of Experts on HIV/AIDS and the World of Work, held in Geneva from 14 to 22 May 2001. It provides invaluable practical guidance to policy-makers, employers' and workers' organizations and other social partners for formulating and implementing appropriate workplace policy, prevention and care programmes, and for establishing strategies to address workers in the informal sector. This is an important ILO contribution to the global effort to fight HIV/AIDS.

The code will help to secure conditions of decent work in the face of a major humanitarian and development crisis. Already, valuable lessons have been learned in attempting to deal with this crisis. A few countries have achieved a degree of success in slowing down the spread of the infection and mitigating its effects on individuals and their communities. The best practices have included committed leadership, multi-sectoral approaches, partnership with civil society, including people living with HIV/AIDS, and education. These elements are reflected in the key principles of the code and its reliance on the mobilization of the social partners for effective implementation.

This is a forward-looking and pioneering document which addresses present problems and anticipates future consequences of the epidemic and its impact on the world of work. Through this code, the ILO will increase its support for international and national commitments to protect the rights and dignity of workers and all people living with HIV/AIDS.

Geneva, June 2001   Juan Somavia,
Director-General.

Participants to the meeting

Experts nominated by governments:

Mr. C.A. de Oliveira Aleixo, Labour Inspector, Ministry of Labour and Employment, Porto Alegre (Brazil).

Advisers:

Dr. M. Fatima Alencar Fernandes D'Assunção, Occupational Medical Officer and Labour Inspector, Ministry of Labour and Employment, Natal (Brazil).

Mr. P. Junqueira-Aguiar, Consultant, Ministry of Health, Brasilia (Brazil).

Ms. X. Lu, Deputy Director, Multilateral Cooperation, Department of International Cooperation, Ministry of Labour and Social Security, Beijing (China).

Mr. U.K. Varma, Chairperson, V.V. Giri National Labour Institute, Noida (India).

Dr. R. Rehayem, Expert: Occupational Health and Safety, Ministry of Labour, Beyrouth (Lebanon).

Mr. P.O. Okwulehie, Assistant Director and Desk Officer HIV/AIDS, Federal Ministry of Employment, Labour and Productivity, Abuja (Nigeria).

Mr. V. Stepanov, Chief of Branch, Ministry of Labour and Social Development, Moscow (Russian Federation).

Mr. C. Faye, Chief, Safety and Health Division, Ministry of Public Administration, Labour and Employment, Dakar (Senegal).

Ms. L. Seftel, Senior Executive Manager, Department of Labour, Pretoria (South Africa).

Dr. L. Aringer, Medical Expert, Organizational and Medical Division, Swedish Work Environment Authority, Solna (Sweden).

Dr. C. Chavalitinitkul, Senior Expert on Occupational Safety and Health, Department of Labour Protection and Welfare, Ministry of Labour and Social Welfare, Bangkok (Thailand).

Dr. S. Onyango, Senior Medical Officer, STD/ACP Ministry of Health, Kampala (Uganda).

Mr. P. Mamacos, Policy Adviser to the Global HIV/AIDS Program, US Department of Labor, Washington, DC (United States).

Advisers:

> Mr. R. Hagen, Permanent Mission of the United States of America to International Organizations and US Information Service, Geneva (Switzerland).

> Ms. R. Saunders, Public Health Adviser, US Centers for Disease Control and Prevention, American Center for International Labor Solidarity, Johannesburg (South Africa).

Experts nominated by the Employers:

Mr. J. Bates, Senior Industry Resources Adviser, Australian Entertainment Industry Association, Melbourne (Australia).

Ms. O. Ngarmbatina, President of the Governing Body, PCA, LABO-REX, National Council of Chadian Employers (CNPT), N'djamena (Chad).

Dr. K. Wahby, Medical Consultant, Ocean Energy, Oil Company, Egyptian Federation of Industries (EFI), Cairo (Egypt).

Dr. A. Harwerth, Corporate Medical Doctor, Daimler Chrysler AG Werk, Bremen (Germany).

Dr. R. Laroche, Vice-President for Social Affairs, Association of Haitian Industries (ADIH), Port-au-Prince (Haiti).

Dr. M.J. Brumas Gozaine, Director, National Council of Private Enterprise (CONEP), Ancon (Panama).

Dr. L. La Grange, Health Adviser, Business South Africa, Chamber of Mines of South Africa, Johannesburg (South Africa).

Mr. E. Jannerfeldt, Medical Adviser, Confederation of Swedish Enterprise, Stockholm (Sweden).

VIII

Mr. C. Katorogo, Training/Marketing Officer in charge of HIV/AIDS Activities, Federation of Uganda Employers (FUE), Kampala (Uganda).

Mr. B. Moats, Corporate Vice-President, Government Affairs, Levi Strauss & Co, San Francisco (United States).

Mr. D. Zulu, Research Specialist, Zambia Federation of Employers (ZFE), Lusaka (Zambia).

Mr. J.W. Mufukare, Executive Director, Employers' Confederation of Zimbabwe, Harare (Zimbabwe).

Experts nominated by the Workers:

Mr. T. Keenan, General Secretary, Victorian Independent Education Union, Melbourne (Australia).

Ms. R. de Cássia Evaristo, Executive Director, Single Central Organization of Workers, São Paulo (Brazil).

Dr. I.A. Kokalov, President, Trade Union Federation (FTU-HS), Health Services, Sofia (Bulgaria).

Mr. P. Saint-Preux, Secretary-General, National Teaching Council of Haiti (CONEH), Port-au-Prince (Haiti).

Mr. S.M. Kanchustambam, General Secretary, South Eastern Railwaymen's Congress (SERMC), Calcutta (India).

Professor R. Aboutaïeb, Member of the Executive Council and Chief, Centre of Studies and Research, General Union of Workers of Morocco (UGTM), Casablanca (Morocco).

Mr. S. Badiane, Section Chief, Grand Yoff General Hospital, Dakar (Senegal).

Ms. C. Ching, Director, Economic and Social Policy Department, International Confederation of Free Trade Unions (ICFTU), Asia and Pacific Regional Organization, Singapore (Singapore).

Mr. S. Wayuphak, Vice President of Labour Congress of Thailand (LCT), Angthong (Thailand).

Ms. T. Kazarina, Chairperson, Central Committee of the Union of Health Workers of Ukraine (CCHWU), Kiev (Ukraine).

Mr. B. Barth, Senior Section Assistant, Education Department, International Transport Workers' Federation (ITF), London (United Kingdom).

Ms. J.D. Lenoir, Assistant Director, AFL-CIO, International Affairs Department, Washington, DC (United States).

International, governmental and non-governmental organizations represented:

Joint United Nations Programme on HIV/AIDS (UNAIDS).

United Nations Education, Scientific, and Cultural Organization (UNESCO).

African Development Bank.

International Organisation of Employers (IOE).

International Confederation of Free Trade Unions (ICFTU).

Organization of African Trade Union Unity (OATUU).

World Confederation of Labour (WCL).

Education International (EI).

Public Services International (PSI).

ILO representatives:

Dr. Franklyn Lisk, Director, ILO Global Programme on HIV/AIDS and the World of Work.

Mr. Behrouz Shahandeh, Senior Adviser on Drugs and Alcohol.

Ms. Jane Hodges, Senior Labour Law Specialist.

Dr. Benjamin O. Alli, Senior Specialist, Operations/Technical Cooperation, ILO Global Programme on HIV/AIDS and the World of Work.

Contents

1. Objective

The objective of this code is to provide a set of guidelines to address the HIV/AIDS epidemic in the world of work and within the framework of the promotion of decent work. The guidelines cover the following key areas of action:

(a) prevention of HIV/AIDS;
(b) management and mitigation of the impact of HIV/AIDS on the world of work;
(c) care and support of workers infected and affected by HIV/AIDS;
(d) elimination of stigma and discrimination on the basis of real or perceived HIV status.

2. Use

This code should be used to:

(a) develop concrete responses at enterprise, community, regional, sectoral, national and international levels;

(b) promote processes of dialogue, consultations, negotiations and all forms of cooperation between governments, employers and workers and their representatives, occupational health personnel, specialists in HIV/AIDS issues, and all relevant stakeholders (which may include community-based and non-governmental organizations (NGOs));

(c) give effect to its contents in consultation with the social partners:

–   in national laws, policies and programmes of action,

–   in workplace/enterprise agreements, and

–   in workplace policies and plans of action.

3. Scope and terms used in the code

3.1. Scope

This code applies to:

(a) all employers and workers (including applicants for work) in the public and private sectors; and

(b) all aspects of work, formal and informal.

3.2. Terms used in the code

HIV: the Human Immunodeficiency Virus, a virus that weakens the body's immune system, ultimately causing AIDS.

Affected persons: persons whose lives are changed in any way by HIV/AIDS due to the broader impact of this epidemic.

AIDS: the Acquired Immune Deficiency Syndrome, a cluster of medical conditions, often referred to as opportunistic infections and cancers and for which, to date, there is no cure.

Discrimination is used in this code in accordance with the definition given in the Discrimination (Employment and Occupation) Convention, 1958 (No. 111), to include HIV status. It also includes discrimination on the basis of a worker's perceived HIV status, including discrimination on the ground of sexual orientation.

Persons with disabilities is used in this code in accordance with the definition given in the Vocational Rehabilitation and Employment (Disabled Persons) Convention, 1983 (No. 159), namely individuals whose prospects of securing, retaining and advancing in suitable employment are substantially reduced as a result of a duly recognized physical or mental impairment.

Employer: a person or organization employing workers under a written or verbal contract of employment which establishes the rights and duties of both parties, in accordance with national law and practice. Governments, public authorities, private enterprises and individuals may be employers.

Occupational health services (OHS) is used in this code in accordance with the description given in the Occupational Health Services Convention, 1985 (No. 161), namely health services which have an essentially preventative function and which are responsible for advising the employer, as well as workers and their representatives, on the requirements for establishing and maintaining a safe and healthy working environment and work methods to facilitate optimal physical and mental health in relation to work. The OHS also provide advice on the adaptation of work to the capabilities of workers in the light of their physical and mental health.

Reasonable accommodation: any modification or adjustment to a job or to the workplace that is reasonably practicable and will enable a person living with HIV or AIDS to have access to or participate or advance in employment.

Screening: measures whether direct (HIV testing), indirect (assessment of risk-taking behaviour) or asking questions about tests already taken or about medication.

Sex and gender: there are both biological and social differences between men and women. The term "sex" refers to biologically determined differences, while the term "gender" refers to differences in social roles and relations between men and women. Gender roles are learned through socialization and vary widely within and between cultures. Gender roles are affected by age, class, race, ethnicity and religion, and by the geographical, economic and political environment.

STI: sexually transmitted infection, which includes, among others, syphilis, chancroid, chlamydia, gonorrhoea. It also includes conditions commonly known as sexually transmitted diseases (STDs).

Termination of employment has the meaning attributed in the Termination of Employment Convention, 1982 (No. 158), namely dismissal at the initiative of the employer.

Universal Precautions are a simple standard of infection control practice to be used to minimize the risk of blood-borne pathogens (see full explanation in Appendix II).

Workers in informal activities (also known as informal sector): this term is described in Appendix I.

Workers' representatives, in accordance with the Workers' Representatives Convention, 1971 (No. 135), are persons recognized as such by national law or practice whether they are:

(a) trade union representatives, namely, representatives designated or elected by trade unions or by members of such unions; or

(b) elected representatives, namely, representatives who are freely elected by the workers of the undertaking in accordance with provisions of national laws or regulations or of collective agreements and whose functions do not include activities which are recognized as the exclusive prerogative of trade unions in the country concerned.

Vulnerability refers to socio-economic disempowerment and cultural context, work situations that make workers more susceptible to the risk of infection and situations which put children at greater risk of being involved in child labour (for more detail see Appendix I).

4. Key principles

4.1. Recognition of HIV/AIDS as a workplace issue

HIV/AIDS is a workplace issue, and should be treated like any other serious illness/ condition in the workplace. This is necessary not only because it affects the workforce, but also because the workplace, being part of the local community, has a role to play in the wider struggle to limit the spread and effects of the epidemic.

4.2. Non-discrimination

In the spirit of decent work and respect for the human rights and dignity of persons infected or affected by HIV/AIDS, there should be no discrimination against workers on the basis of real or perceived HIV status. Discrimination and stigmatization of people living with HIV/AIDS inhibits efforts aimed at promoting HIV/AIDS prevention.

4.3. Gender equality

The gender dimensions of HIV/AIDS should be recognized. Women are more likely to become infected and are more often adversely affected by the HIV/AIDS epidemic than men for biological, socio-cultural and economic reasons. The greater the gender discrimination in societies and the lower the position of women, the more negatively they are affected by HIV. Therefore, more equal gender relations and the empowerment of women are vital to successfully prevent the spread of HIV infection and enable women to cope with HIV/AIDS.

4.4. Healthy work environment

The work environment should be healthy and safe, so far as is practicable, for all concerned parties, in order to prevent transmission of HIV, in accordance with the provisions of the Occupational Safety and Health Convention, 1981 (No. 155).

A healthy work environment facilitates optimal physical and mental health in relation to work and adaptation of work to the capabilities of workers in light of their state of physical and mental health.

4.5. Social dialogue

The successful implementation of an HIV/AIDS policy and programme requires cooperation and trust between employers, workers and their representatives and government, where appropriate, with the active involvement of workers infected and affected by HIV/AIDS.

4.6. Screening for purposes of exclusion from employment or work processes

HIV/AIDS screening should not be required of job applicants or persons in employment.

4.7. Confidentiality

There is no justification for asking job applicants or workers to disclose HIV-related personal information. Nor should co-workers be obliged to reveal such personal information about fellow workers. Access to personal data relating to a worker's HIV status should be bound by the rules of confidentiality consistent with the ILO's code of practice on the protection of workers' personal data, 1997.

4.8. Continuation of employment relationship

HIV infection is not a cause for termination of employment. As with many other conditions, persons with HIV-related illnesses should be able to work for as long as medically fit in available, appropriate work.

4.9. Prevention

HIV infection is preventable. Prevention of all means of transmission can be achieved through a variety of strategies which are appropriately targeted to national conditions and which are culturally sensitive.

Prevention can be furthered through changes in behaviour, knowledge, treatment and the creation of a non-discriminatory environment.

The social partners are in a unique position to promote prevention efforts, particularly in relation to changing attitudes and behaviours, through the provision of information and education, and in addressing socio-economic factors.

4.10. Care and support

Solidarity, care and support should guide the response to HIV/AIDS in the world of work. All workers, including workers with HIV, are entitled to affordable health services. There should be no discrimination against them and their dependants in access to and receipt of benefits from statutory social security programmes and occupational schemes.

5. General rights and responsibilities

5.1. Governments and their competent authorities

(a) *Coherence.* Governments should ensure coherence in national HIV/AIDS strategy and programmes, recognizing the importance of including the world of work in national plans, for example by ensuring that the composition of national AIDS councils includes representatives of employers, workers, people living with HIV/AIDS and of ministries responsible for labour and social matters.

(b) *Multi-sectoral participation.* The competent authorities should mobilize and support broad partnerships for protection and prevention, including public agencies, the private sector, workers' and employers' organizations, and all relevant stakeholders, so that the greatest number of partners in the world of work are involved.

(c) *Coordination.* Governments should facilitate and coordinate all interventions at the national level that provide an enabling environment for world of work interventions and capitalize on the presence of the social partners and all relevant stakeholders. Coordination should build on measures and support services already in place.

(d) *Prevention and health promotion.* The competent authorities should instigate and work in partnership with other social partners to promote awareness and prevention programmes, particularly in the workplace.

(e) *Clinical guidelines.* In countries where employers assume a primary responsibility for providing direct health-care services to workers, governments should offer guidelines to assist employers in the care and clinical management of HIV/AIDS. These guidelines should take account of existing services.

(f) *Social protection.* Governments should ensure that benefits under national laws and regulations apply to workers with HIV/AIDS no less favourably than to workers with other serious illnesses. In designing and implementing social security programmes, governments should take into account the progressive and intermittent nature of the disease and tailor schemes accordingly, for example by making benefits available as and when needed and by the expeditious treatment of claims.

(g) *Research.* In order to achieve coherence with national AIDS plans, to mobilize the social partners, to evaluate the costs of the epidemic on workplaces, for the social security system and for the economy, and to facilitate planning to mitigate its socio-economic impact, the competent authorities should encourage, support, carry out and publish the findings of demographic projections, incidence and prevalence studies and case studies of best practice. Governments should endeavour to provide the institutional and regulatory framework to achieve this. The research should include gender-sensitive analyses that make use of research and data from employers and their organizations and workers' organizations. Data collection should, to the extent possible, be sector-specific and disaggregated by sex, race, sexual orientation, age, employment and occupational status and be done in a culturally sensitive manner. Where possible, permanent impact assessment mechanisms should exist.

(h) *Financial resourcing.* Governments, where possible, in consultation with the social partners and other stakeholders, should estimate the financial implications of HIV/AIDS and seek to mobilize funding locally and internationally for their national AIDS strategic plans including, where relevant, for their social security systems.

(i) *Legislation.* In order to eliminate workplace discrimination and ensure workplace prevention and social protection, governments, in consultation with the social partners and experts in the field of HIV/AIDS, should provide the relevant regulatory framework and, where necessary, revise labour laws and other legislation.

(j) *Conditionalities for government support.* When governments provide start-up funding and incentives for national and international enterprises, they should require recipients to adhere to national laws and encourage recipients to adhere to this code, and policies or codes that give effect to the provisions of this code.

(k) *Enforcement.* The competent authorities should supply technical information and advice to employers and workers concerning the most effective way of complying with legislation and regulations applicable to HIV/AIDS and the world of work. They should strengthen enforcement structures and procedures, such as factory/labour inspectorates and labour courts and tribunals.

(l) *Workers in informal activities (also known as informal sector).* Governments should extend and adapt their HIV/AIDS prevention programmes to such workers including income generation and social protection. Governments should also design and develop new approaches using local communities where appropriate.

(m) *Mitigation.* Governments should promote care and support through public health-care programmes, social security systems and/or other relevant government initiatives. Governments should also strive to ensure access to treatment and, where appropriate, to work in partnership with employers and workers' organizations.

(n) *Children and young persons.* In programmes to eliminate child labour, governments should ensure that attention is paid to the impact of the epidemic on children and young persons whose parent or parents are ill or have died as a result of HIV/AIDS.

(o) *Regional and international collaboration.* Governments should promote and support collaboration at regional and international levels, and through intergovernmental agencies and all relevant stakeholders, so as to focus international attention on HIV/AIDS and on the related needs of the world of work.

(p) *International assistance.* Governments should enlist international assistance where appropriate in support of national programmes. They should encourage initiatives aimed at supporting international campaigns to reduce the cost of, and improve access to, antiretroviral drugs.

(q) *Vulnerability.* Governments should take measures to identify groups of workers who are vulnerable to infection, and adopt strategies to overcome the factors that make these workers susceptible. Governments should also endeavour to ensure that appropriate prevention programmes are in place for these workers.

5.2. Employers and their organizations

(a) *Workplace policy.* Employers should consult with workers and their representatives to develop and implement an appropriate policy for their workplace, designed to prevent the spread of the infection and protect all workers from discrimination related to HIV/AIDS. A checklist for workplace policy planning and implementation appears in Appendix III.

(b) *National, sectoral and workplace/enterprise agreements.* Employers should adhere to national law and practice in relation to negotiating terms and conditions of employment about HIV/AIDS issues with workers and their representatives, and endeavour to include provisions on HIV/AIDS protection and prevention in national, sectoral and workplace/enterprise agreements.

(c) *Education and training.* Employers and their organizations, in consultation with workers and their representatives, should initiate and support programmes at their workplaces to inform, educate and train workers about HIV/AIDS prevention, care and support and the enterprise's policy on HIV/AIDS, including measures to reduce discrimination against people infected or affected by HIV/AIDS and specific staff benefits and entitlements.

(d) *Economic impact.* Employers, workers and their organizations, should work together to develop appropriate strategies to assess and appropriately respond to the economic impact of HIV/AIDS on their particular workplace and sector.

(e) *Personnel policies.* Employers should not engage in nor permit any personnel policy or practice that discriminates against workers infected with or affected by HIV/AIDS. In particular, employers should:

– not require HIV/AIDS screening or testing unless otherwise specified in section 8 of this code;

– ensure that work is performed free of discrimination or stigmatization based on perceived or real HIV status;

> – encourage persons with HIV and AIDS-related illnesses to work as long as medically fit for appropriate work; and

> – provide that, where a worker with an AIDS-related condition is too ill to continue to work and where alternative working arrangements including extended sick leave have been exhausted, the employment relationship may cease in accordance with anti-discrimination and labour laws and respect for general procedures and full benefits.

(f) *Grievance and disciplinary procedures.* Employers should have procedures that can be used by workers and their representatives for work-related grievances. These procedures should specify under what circumstances disciplinary proceedings can be commenced against any employee who discriminates on the grounds of real or perceived HIV status or who violates the workplace policy on HIV/AIDS.

(g) *Confidentiality.* HIV/AIDS-related information of workers should be kept strictly confidential and kept only on medical files, whereby access to information complies with the Occupational Health Services Recommendation, 1985 (No. 171), and national laws and practices. Access to such information should be strictly limited to medical personnel and such information may only be disclosed if legally required or with the consent of the person concerned.

(h) *Risk reduction and management.* Employers should ensure a safe and healthy working environment, including the application of Universal Precautions and measures such as the provision and maintenance of protective equipment and first aid. To support behavioural change by individuals, employers should also make available, where appropriate, male and female condoms, counselling, care, support and referral services. Where size and cost considerations make this difficult, employers and/or their organizations should seek support from government and other relevant institutions.

(i) *Workplaces where workers come into regular contact with human blood and body fluids.* In such workplaces, employers need to take additional measures to ensure that all workers are trained in Universal Precautions, that they are knowledgeable about procedures to be followed in the event of an occupational incident and that Universal Precautions are always observed. Facilities should be provided for these measures.

(j) *Reasonable accommodation.* Employers, in consultation with the worker(s) and their representatives, should take measures to reasonably accommodate the worker(s) with AIDS-related illnesses. These could include rearrangement of working time, special equipment, opportunities for rest breaks, time off for medical appointments, flexible sick leave, part-time work and return-to-work arrangements.

(k) *Advocacy.* In the spirit of good corporate citizenship, employers and their organizations should, where appropriate, encourage fellow employers to contribute to the prevention and management of HIV/AIDS in the workplace, and encourage governments to take all necessary action to stop the spread of HIV/AIDS and mitigate its effects. Other partnerships can support this process such as joint business/trade union councils on HIV/AIDS.

(l) *Support for confidential voluntary HIV counselling and testing.* Employers, workers and their representatives should encourage support for, and access to, confidential voluntary counselling and testing that is provided by qualified health services.

15

(m) *Workers in informal activities (also known as informal sector).* Employers of workers in informal activities should investigate and, where appropriate, develop prevention and care programmes for these workers.

(n) *International partnerships.* Employers and their organizations should contribute, where appropriate, to international partnerships in the fight against HIV/AIDS.

5.3. Workers and their organizations

(a) *Workplace policy.* Workers and their representatives should consult with their employers on the implementation of an appropriate policy for their workplace, designed to prevent the spread of the infection and protect all workers from discrimination related to HIV/AIDS. A checklist for workplace policy planning and implementation appears in Appendix III.

(b) *National, sectoral and workplace/enterprise agreements.* Workers and their organizations should adhere to national law and practice when negotiating terms and conditions of employment relating to HIV/AIDS issues, and endeavour to include provisions on HIV/AIDS protection and prevention in national, sectoral and workplace/enterprise agreements.

(c) *Information and education.* Workers and their organizations should use existing union structures and other structures and facilities to provide information on HIV/AIDS in the workplace, and develop educational materials and activities appropriate for workers and their families, including regularly updated information on workers' rights and benefits.

(d) *Economic impact*. Workers and their organizations should work together with employers to develop appropriate strategies to assess and appropriately respond to the economic impact of HIV/AIDS in their particular workplace and sector.

(e) *Advocacy*. Workers and their organizations should work with employers, their organizations and governments to raise awareness of HIV/AIDS prevention and management.

(f) *Personnel policies.* Workers and their representatives should support and encourage employers in creating and implementing personnel policy and practices that do not discriminate against workers with HIV/AIDS.

(g) *Monitoring of compliance.* Workers' representatives have the right to take up issues at their workplaces through grievance and disciplinary procedures and/or should report all discrimination on the basis of HIV/AIDS to the appropriate legal authorities.

(h) *Training*. Workers' organizations should develop and carry out training courses for their representatives on workplace issues raised by the epidemic, on appropriate responses, and on the general needs of people living with HIV/AIDS and their carers.

(i) *Risk reduction and management*. Workers and their organizations should advocate for, and cooperate with, employers to maintain a safe and healthy working environment, including the correct application and maintenance of protective equipment and first aid. Workers and their organizations should assess the vulnerability of the working environment and promote tailored programmes for workers as appropriate.

(j) *Confidentiality*. Workers have the right to access their own personal and medical files. Workers' organizations should not have access to personnel data relating to a worker's HIV status. In all cases, when carrying out trade union responsibilities and functions, the rules of confidentiality and the requirement for the concerned person's consent set out in the Occupational Health Services Recommendation, 1985 (No. 171), should apply.

(k) *Workers in informal activities (also known as informal sector)*. Workers and their organizations should extend their activities to these workers in partnership with all other relevant stakeholders, where appropriate, and support new initiatives which help both prevent the spread of HIV/AIDS and mitigate its impact.

(l) *Vulnerability*. Workers and their organizations should ensure that factors that increase the risk of infection for certain groups of workers are addressed in consultation with employers.

(m) *Support for confidential voluntary HIV counselling and testing*. Workers and their organizations should work with employers to encourage and support access to confidential voluntary counselling and testing.

(n) *International partnerships*. Workers' organizations should build solidarity across national borders by using sectoral, regional and international groupings to highlight HIV/AIDS and the world of work, and to include it in workers' rights campaigns.

6. Prevention through information and education

Workplace information and education programmes are essential to combat the spread of the epidemic and to foster greater tolerance for workers with HIV/AIDS. Effective education can contribute to the capacity of workers to protect themselves against HIV infection. It can significantly reduce HIV-related anxiety and stigmatization, minimize disruption in the workplace, and bring about attitudinal and behavioural change. Programmes should be developed through consultations between governments, employers and workers and their representatives to ensure support at the highest levels and the fullest participation of all concerned. Information and education should be provided in a variety of forms, not relying exclusively on the written word and including distance learning where necessary. Programmes should be targeted and tailored to the age, gender, sexual orientation, sectoral characteristics and behavioural risk factors of the workforce and its cultural context. They should be delivered by trusted and respected individuals. Peer education has been found to be particularly effective, as has the involvement of people living with HIV/AIDS in the design and implementation of programmes.

6.1. Information and awareness-raising campaigns

(a) Information programmes should, where possible, be linked to broader HIV/AIDS campaigns within the local community, sector, region or country. The programmes should be based on correct and up-to-date information about how HIV is and is not transmitted, dispel the myths surrounding HIV/AIDS, how HIV can be prevented, medical aspects of the disease, the impact of AIDS on individuals, and the possibilities for care, support and treatment.

19

(b) As far as is practicable, information programmes, courses and campaigns should be integrated into existing education and human resource policies and programmes as well as occupational safety and health and anti-discrimination strategies.

6.2. Educational programmes

(a) Educational strategies should be based on consultation between employers and workers, and their representatives and, where appropriate, government and other relevant stakeholders with expertise in HIV/AIDS education, counselling and care. The methods should be as interactive and participatory as possible.

(b) Consideration should be given to educational programmes taking place during paid working hours and developing educational materials to be used by workers outside workplaces. Where courses are offered, attendance should be considered as part of work obligations.

(c) Where practical and appropriate, programmes should:
  - include activities to help individuals assess the risks that face them personally (both as individuals and as members of a group) and reduce these risks through decision-making, negotiation and communication skills, as well as educational, preventative and counselling programmes;
  - give special emphasis to high-risk behaviour and other risk factors such as occupational mobility that expose certain groups of workers to increased risk of HIV infection;
  - provide information about transmission of HIV through drug injection and information about how to reduce the risk of such transmission;

- enhance dialogue among governments and employers' and workers' organizations from neighbouring countries and at regional level;
- promote HIV/AIDS awareness in vocational training programmes carried out by governments and enterprises, in collaboration with workers' organizations;
- promote campaigns targeted at young workers and women;
- give special emphasis to the vulnerability of women to HIV and prevention strategies that can lessen this vulnerability (see section 6.3);
- emphasize that HIV cannot be contracted through casual contact, and that people who are HIV-positive do not need to be avoided or stigmatized, but rather should be supported and accommodated in the workplace;
- explain the debilitating effects of the virus and the need for all workers to be empathetic and non-discriminatory towards workers with HIV/AIDS;
- give workers the opportunity to express and discuss their reactions and emotions caused by HIV/AIDS;
- instruct workers (especially health-care workers) on the use of Universal Precautions and inform them of procedures to be followed in case of exposure;
- provide education about the prevention and management of STIs and tuberculosis, not only because of the associated risk of HIV infection but also because these conditions are treatable, thus improving the workers' general health and immunity;
- promote hygiene and proper nutrition;

- – promote safer sex practices, including instructions on the use of male and female condoms;
- – encourage peer education and informal education activities;
- – be regularly monitored, evaluated, reviewed and revised where necessary.

6.3. Gender-specific programmes

(a) All programmes should be gender-sensitive, as well as sensitive to race and sexual orientation. This includes targeting both women and men explicitly, or addressing either women or men in separate programmes, in recognition of the different types and degrees of risk for men and women workers.

(b) Information for women needs to alert them to, and explain their higher risk of, infection, in particular the special vulnerability of young women.

(c) Education should help both women and men to understand and act upon the unequal power relations between them in employment and personal situations; harassment and violence should be addressed specifically.

(d) Programmes should help women to understand their rights, both within the workplace and outside it, and empower them to protect themselves.

(e) Education for men should include awareness-raising, risk assessment and strategies to promote men's responsibilities regarding HIV/AIDS prevention.

(f) Appropriately targeted prevention programmes should be developed for homosexually active men in consultation with these workers and their representatives.

6.4. Linkage to health promotion programmes

Educational programmes should be linked, where feasible, to health promotion programmes dealing with issues such as substance abuse, stress and reproductive health at the workplace. Existing work councils or health and safety committees provide an entry point to HIV/AIDS awareness campaigns and educational programmes. This linkage should highlight the increased risk of infection in the use of contaminated needles in intravenous drug-injection. It should also highlight that intoxication due to alcohol and drugs could lead to behaviour which increases the risk of HIV infection.

6.5. Practical measures to support behavioural change

(a) Workers should be provided with sensitive, accurate and up-to-date education about risk reduction strategies, and, where appropriate, male and female condoms should be made available.

(b) Early and effective STI and tuberculosis diagnosis, treatment and management, as well as a sterile needle and syringe-exchange programmes, should also be made available, where appropriate, or information provided on where they can be obtained.

(c) For women workers in financial need, education should include strategies to supplement low incomes, for example, by supplying information on income-generating activities, tax relief and wage support.

6.6. Community outreach programmes

Employers, workers and their representatives should encourage and promote information and education programmes on prevention and management of HIV/AIDS within the local community, especially in schools. Participation in outreach programmes should be encouraged in order to provide an opportunity for people to express their views and enhance the welfare of workers with HIV/AIDS by reducing their isolation and ostracism. Such programmes should be run in partnership with appropriate national or local bodies.

7. Training

Training should be targeted at, and adapted to, the different groups being trained: managers, supervisors and personnel officers; workers and their representatives; trainers of trainers (both male and female); peer educators; occupational health and safety officers; and factory/labour inspectors. Innovative approaches should be sought to defray costs. For example, enterprises can seek external support from national AIDS programmes or other relevant stakeholders by borrowing instructors or having their own trained. Training materials can vary enormously, according to available resources. They can be adapted to local customs and to the different circumstances of women and men. Trainers should also be trained to deal with prejudices against minorities, especially in relation to ethnic origin or sexual orientation. They should draw on case studies and available good practice materials. The best trainers are often staff themselves and peer education is therefore recommended at all levels. It should become part of a workplace's annual training plan, which should be developed in consultation with workers' representatives.

7.1. Training for managers, supervisors and personnel officers

In addition to participating in information and education programmes that are directed at all workers, supervisory and managerial personnel should receive training to:

– enable them to explain and respond to questions about the workplace's HIV/AIDS policy;
– be well informed about HIV/AIDS so as to help other workers overcome misconceptions about the spread of HIV/AIDS at the workplace;

- explain reasonable accommodation options to workers with HIV/AIDS so as to enable them to continue to work as long as possible;

- identify and manage workplace behaviour, conduct or practices which discriminate against or alienate workers with HIV/AIDS;

- enable them to advise about the health services and social benefits which are available.

7.2. Training for peer educators

Peer educators should receive specialized training so as to:

- be sufficiently knowledgeable about the content and methods of HIV/AIDS prevention so that they can deliver, in whole or in part, the information and education programme to the workforce;

- be sensitive to race, sexual orientation, gender and culture in developing and delivering their training;

- link into and draw from other existing workplace policies, such as those on sexual harassment or for persons with disabilities in the workplace;

- enable their co-workers to identify factors in their lives that lead to increased risk of infection;

- be able to counsel workers living with HIV/AIDS about coping with their condition and its implications.

7.3. Training for workers' representatives

Workers' representatives should, during paid working hours, receive training so as to:

- enable them to explain and respond to questions about the workplace HIV/AIDS policy;
- enable them to train other workers in trainer education programmes;
- identify individual workplace behaviour, conduct or practices which discriminate or alienate workers with HIV/AIDS, in order to effectively combat such conduct;
- help and represent workers with AIDS-related illnesses to access reasonable accommodation when so requested;
- be able to counsel workers to identify and reduce risk factors in their personal lives;
- be well instructed about HIV/AIDS in order to inform workers about the spread of HIV/AIDS;
- ensure that any information that they acquire about workers with HIV/AIDS in the course of performing their representative functions is kept confidential.

7.4. Training for health and safety officers

In addition to becoming familiar with the information and education programmes that are directed at all workers, health and safety officers should receive specialized training in order to:

- be sufficiently knowledgeable about the content and methods of HIV/AIDS prevention so that they can deliver information and education programmes to workers;
- be able to assess the working environment and identify working methods or conditions which could be changed or improved in order to lessen the vulnerability of workers with HIV/AIDS;

– verify whether the employer provides and maintains a healthy and safe working environment and processes for the workers, including safe first-aid procedures;

– ensure that HIV/AIDS-related information, if any, is maintained under conditions of strict confidentiality as with other medical data pertinent to workers and disclosed only in accordance with the ILO's code of practice on the protection of workers' personal data;

– be able to counsel workers to identify and reduce risk factors in their personal lives;

– be able to refer workers to in-house medical services or those outside the workplace which can effectively respond to their needs.

7.5. Training for factory/labour inspectors

The competent authority should ensure that factory and labour inspectors have sufficient means at their disposal to fulfil their supervisory, enforcement and advisory functions, in particular regarding HIV/AIDS prevention in enterprises. To achieve this, they should receive specialized training on HIV/AIDS prevention and protection strategies at the workplace. This training should include:

– information on relevant international labour standards, especially the Discrimination (Employment and Occupation) Convention, 1958 (No. 111), and national laws and regulations;

– how to provide awareness about HIV/AIDS to workers and management;

- how to incorporate HIV/AIDS topics into their regular occupational safety and health briefings and workplace training;
- how to assist workers to access available benefits (such as how to complete benefit forms) and to exercise other legal rights;
- how to identify violations, or the lack of implementation of, workers' rights in respect of HIV status;
- skills to collect and analyse data relating to HIV/AIDS in workplaces when this is for epidemiological or social impact studies and in conformity with this code.

7.6. Training for workers who come into contact with human blood and other body fluids

All workers should receive training about infection control procedures in the context of workplace accidents and first aid. The programmes should provide training:

- in the provision of first aid;
- about Universal Precautions to reduce the risk of exposure to human blood and other body fluids (see Appendix II);
- in the use of protective equipment;
- in the correct procedures to be followed in the event of exposure to human blood or body fluids;
- about rights to compensation in the event of an occupational incident.

and emphasize that the taking of precautions is not necessarily related to the perceived or actual HIV status of individuals.

8. Testing

Testing for HIV should not be carried out at the workplace except as specified in this code. It is unnecessary and imperils the human rights and dignity of workers: test results may be revealed and misused, and the informed consent of workers may not always be fully free or based on an appreciation of all the facts and implications of testing. Even outside the workplace, confidential testing for HIV should be the consequence of voluntary informed consent and performed by suitably qualified personnel only, in conditions of the strictest confidentiality.

8.1. Prohibition in recruitment and employment

HIV testing should not be required at the time of recruitment or as a condition of continued employment. Any routine medical testing, such as testing for fitness carried out prior to the commencement of employment or on a regular basis for workers, should not include mandatory HIV testing.

8.2. Prohibition for insurance purposes

(a) HIV testing should not be required as a condition of eligibility for national social security schemes, general insurance policies, occupational schemes and health insurance.

(b) Insurance companies should not require HIV testing before agreeing to provide coverage for a given workplace. They may base their cost and revenue estimates and their actuarial calculations on available epidemiological data for the general population.

(c) Employers should not facilitate any testing for insurance purposes and all information that they already have should remain confidential.

8.3. Epidemiological surveillance

Anonymous, unlinked surveillance or epidemiological HIV testing in the workplace may occur provided it is undertaken in accordance with the ethical principles of scientific research, professional ethics and the protection of individual rights and confidentiality. Where such research is done, workers and employers should be consulted and informed that it is occurring. The information obtained may not be used to discriminate against individuals or groups of persons. Testing will not be considered anonymous if there is a reasonable possibility that a person's HIV status can be deduced from the results.

8.4. Voluntary testing

There may be situations where workers wish at their own initiative to be tested, including as part of voluntary testing programmes. Voluntary testing should normally be carried out by the community health services and not at the workplace. Where adequate medical services exist, voluntary testing may be undertaken at the request and with the written informed consent of a worker, with advice from the workers' representative if so requested. It should be performed by suitably qualified personnel with adherence to strict confidentiality and disclosure requirements. Gender-sensitive pre- and post-test counselling, which facilitates an understanding of the nature and purpose of the HIV tests, the advantages and disadvantages of the tests and the effect of the result upon the worker, should form an essential part of any testing procedure.

8.5. Tests and treatment after occupational exposure

(a) Where there is a risk of exposure to human blood, body fluids or tissues, the workplace should have procedures in place to manage the risk of such exposure and occupational incidents.

(b) Following risk of exposure to potentially infected material (human blood, body fluids, tissue) at the workplace, the worker should be immediately counselled to cope with the incident, about the medical consequences, the desirability of testing for HIV and the availability of post-exposure prophylaxis, and referred to appropriate medical facilities. Following the conclusion of a risk assessment, further guidance as to the worker's legal rights, including eligibility and required procedures for workers' compensation, should be given.

9. Care and support

Solidarity, care and support are critical elements that should guide a workplace in responding to HIV/AIDS. Mechanisms should be created to encourage openness, acceptance and support for those workers who disclose their HIV status, and ensure that they are not discriminated against nor stigmatized. To mitigate the impact of the HIV/AIDS epidemic in the workplace, workplaces should endeavour to provide counselling and other forms of social support to workers infected and affected by HIV/AIDS. Where health-care services exist at the workplace, appropriate treatment should be provided. Where these services are not possible, workers should be informed about the location of available outside services. Linkages such as this have the advantage of reaching beyond the workers to cover their families, in particular their children. Partnership between governments, employers, workers and their organizations and other relevant stakeholders also ensures effective delivery of services and saves costs.

9.1. Parity with other serious illnesses

(a) HIV infection and clinical AIDS should be managed in the workplace no less favourably than any other serious illness or condition.

(b) Workers with HIV/AIDS should be treated no less favourably than workers with other serious illnesses in terms of benefits, workers' compensation and reasonable accommodation.

(c) As long as workers are medically fit for appropriate employment, they should enjoy normal job security and opportunities for transfer and advancement.

9.2. Counselling

(a) Employers should encourage workers with HIV/AIDS to use expertise and assistance outside the enterprise for counselling or, where available, its own occupational safety and health unit or other workplace programme, if specialized and confidential counselling is offered.

(b) To give effect to this, employers should consider the following actions:

- identify professionals, self-help groups and services within the local community or region which specialize in HIV/AIDS-related counselling and the treatment of HIV/AIDS;

- identify community-based organizations, both of a medical and non-medical character, that may be useful to workers with HIV/AIDS;

- suggest that the worker contact his or her doctor or qualified health-care providers for initial assessment and treatment if not already being treated, or help the worker locate a qualified health-care provider if he or she does not have one.

(c) Employers should provide workers with HIV/AIDS with reasonable time off for counselling and treatment in conformity with minimum national requirements.

(d) Counselling support should be made accessible at no cost to the workers and adapted to the different needs and circumstances of women and men. It may be appropriate to liaise with government, workers and their organizations and other relevant stakeholders in establishing and providing such support.

(e) Workers' representatives should, if requested, assist a worker with HIV/AIDS to obtain professional counselling.

(f) Counselling services should inform all workers of their rights and benefits in relation to statutory social security programmes and occupational schemes and any life-skills programmes which may help workers cope with HIV/AIDS.

(g) In the event of occupational exposure to HIV, employers should provide workers with reasonable paid time off for counselling purposes.

9.3. Occupational and other health services

(a) Some employers may be in a position to assist their workers with access to antiretroviral drugs. Where health services exist at the workplace these should offer, in cooperation with government and all other stakeholders, the broadest range of health services possible to prevent and manage HIV/AIDS and assist workers living with HIV/AIDS.

(b) These services could include the provision of antiretroviral drugs, treatment for the relief of HIV-related symptoms, nutritional counselling and supplements, stress reduction and treatment for the more common opportunistic infections including STIs and tuberculosis.

9.4. Linkages with self-help and community-based groups

Where appropriate, employers, workers' organizations and occupational health personnel should facilitate the establishment of self-help groups within the enterprise or the referral of workers affected by HIV/AIDS to self-help groups and support organizations in the local community.

9.5. Benefits

(a) Governments, in consultation with the social partners, should ensure that benefits under national laws and regulations apply to workers with HIV/AIDS no less favourably than to workers with other serious illnesses. They should also explore the sustainability of new benefits specifically addressing the progressive and intermittent nature of HIV/AIDS.

(b) Employers and employers' and workers' organizations should pursue with governments the adaptation of existing benefit mechanisms to the needs of workers with HIV/AIDS, including wage subsidy schemes.

9.6. Social security coverage

(a) Governments, employers and workers' organizations should take all steps necessary to ensure that workers with HIV/AIDS and their families are not excluded from the full protection and benefits of social security programmes and occupational schemes. This should also apply to workers and their families from occupational and social groups perceived to be at risk of HIV/AIDS.

(b) These programmes and schemes should provide similar benefits for workers with HIV/AIDS as those for workers with other serious illnesses.

9.7. Privacy and confidentiality

(a) Governments, private insurance companies and employers should ensure that information relating to counselling, care, treatment and receipt of benefits is kept confidential, as with medical data pertinent to workers, and accessed only in accordance with the Occupational Health Services Recommendation, 1985 (No. 171).

(b) Third parties, such as trustees and administrators of social security programmes and occupational schemes, should keep all HIV/AIDS-related information confidential, as with medical data pertinent to workers, in accordance with the ILO's code of practice on the protection of workers' personal data.

9.8. Employee and family assistance programmes

(a) In the light of the nature of the epidemic, employee assistance programmes may need to be established or extended appropriately to include a range of services for workers as members of families, and to support their family members. This should be done in consultation with workers and their representatives, and can be done in collaboration with government and other relevant stakeholders in accordance with resources and needs.

(b) Such programmes should recognize that women normally undertake the major part of caring for those with AIDS-related illnesses. They should also recognize the particular needs of pregnant women. They should respond to the needs of children who have lost one or both parents to AIDS, and who may then drop out of school, be forced to work, and become increasingly vulnerable to sexual exploitation. The programmes may be in-house, or enterprises could support such programmes collectively or contract out for such services from an independent enterprise.

(c) The family assistance programme may include:
   - compassionate leave;
   - invitations to participate in information and education programmes;

- referrals to support groups, including self-help groups;
- assistance to families of workers to obtain alternative employment for the worker or family members provided that the work does not interfere with schooling;
- specific measures, such as support for formal education, vocational training and apprenticeships, to meet the needs of children and young persons who have lost one or both parents to AIDS;
- coordination with all relevant stakeholders and community-based organizations including the schools attended by the workers' children;
- direct or indirect financial assistance;
- managing financial issues relating to sickness and the needs of dependants;
- legal information, advice and assistance;
- assistance in relation to understanding the legal processes of illness and death such as managing financial issues relating to sickness, preparation of wills and succession plans;
- helping families to deal with social security programmes and occupational schemes;
- provision of advanced payments due to the worker;
- directing families to the relevant legal and health authorities or providing a list of recommended authorities.

Appendix I

Basic facts about the epidemic and its implications

Facts about HIV and AIDS

The Human Immunodeficiency Virus (HIV) which causes AIDS is transmitted through body fluids – in particular blood, semen, vaginal secretions and breast milk. It has been established that transmission takes place in four ways: unprotected sexual intercourse with an infected partner (the most common); blood and blood products through, for example, infected transfusions and organ or tissue transplants, or the use of contaminated injection or other skin-piercing equipment; transmission from infected mother to child in the womb or at birth; and breastfeeding. HIV is not transmitted by casual physical contact, coughing, sneezing and kissing, by sharing toilet and washing facilities, by using eating utensils or consuming food and beverages handled by someone who has HIV; it is not spread by mosquitoes or other insect bites.

HIV weakens the human body's immune system, making it difficult to fight infection. A person may live for ten years or more after infection, much of this time without symptoms or sickness, although they can still transmit the infection to others. Early symptoms of AIDS include: chronic fatigue, diarrhoea, fever, mental changes such as memory loss, weight loss, persistent cough, severe recurrent skin rashes, herpes and mouth infections, and swelling of the lymph nodes. Opportunistic diseases such as cancers, meningitis, pneumonia and tuberculosis may also take advantage of the body's weakened immune system. Although periods of illness may be interspersed with periods of remission, AIDS is almost always fatal. Research is currently under way into vaccines, but none is viable as yet. Antiretroviral drugs are available that slow the progression of the disease and prolong life; at present these are very expensive and consequently unavailable to most sufferers, but the situation is changing rapidly. HIV is a fragile virus, which can only survive in a limited range of conditions. It can only enter the body through naturally moist places and cannot penetrate unbroken skin. Prevention therefore involves ensuring that there is a barrier to the virus, for example condoms or protective equipment such as gloves and masks (where appropriate), and that skin-piercing equipment is not contaminated; the virus is killed by bleach, strong detergents and very hot water (see Appendix II).

Demographic and labour force impact

At the end of 2000, over 36 million people were living with HIV/AIDS, two-thirds of them in sub-Saharan Africa. Nearly 22 million people have died from AIDS; there were 3 million deaths worldwide for the 12 months of 2000.

All regions are affected: adults and children with HIV/AIDS number over 25 million in sub-Saharan Africa; over 6 million in Asia; nearly 2 million in Latin America and the Caribbean; just under 1 million in North America; half a million in Western Europe; nearly three-quarters of a million in Eastern Europe and Central Asia; nearly half a million in North Africa and the Middle East. Although the dominant mode of transmission may vary, regions are experiencing increased rates of infection.

The consequences of AIDS deaths for total population numbers in Africa are clear: by 2010, for 29 countries with prevalence rates of over 2 per cent, the total population will be 50 million fewer than in the absence of AIDS. There are sex and age consequences as well, as in many countries women often become infected at a younger age than men; in Africa over half of new infections are among women. The age group worst affected everywhere is the 15-49 year-olds, the active population, whose contributions to the family, society and the economy are thus being lost. The ILO estimates that over 20 million workers globally are living with HIV/AIDS. The size of the labour force in high-prevalence countries will be between 10 and 30 per cent smaller by 2020 than it would have been without AIDS; 14 million children have lost one or both parents to AIDS, and many of them will be forced out of school and on to the job market, exacerbating the problem of child labour.

HIV/AIDS has an enormous impact on infected individuals and their families, as well as on the community at large. The implications are serious for the old and young dependants of infected family members. The impact at the individual and household level is mirrored at the enterprise level and, increasingly, in the national economy. The epidemic manifests itself in the world of work in many ways: disruption of production, discrimination in employment, the worsening of gender inequalities, and increased incidence of child labour; other manifestations are depleted human capital, pressure on health and social security systems, and threatened occupational safety and health.

Conditions that contribute to vulnerability

General factors

AIDS thrives where economic, social and cultural rights are violated, and also where civil and political norms are ignored. On the economic side, poverty merits highlighting as a major factor: the illiteracy and marginalization of the poor make them more vulnerable to infection, and poverty puts pressure on women to survive and support their families by engaging in unsafe sex. Poor diet, inadequate housing and lack of hygiene make HIV-infected persons even more vulnerable to AIDS-related diseases. On the social and cultural side, inequality in personal and working relations leads to unwanted sex in conditions of risk. Attitudes and behaviour should also be recognized as factors that may increase risk. HIV may be transmitted through injecting intravenous drugs with contaminated equipment. There is also evidence that drug and alcohol abuse can impair an individual's ability to practice safe sexual and injecting behaviour. The stigmatization of people living with HIV/AIDS fuels a natural desire to keep quiet about infection, thus helping its spread. Cultural pressures and denial mask the extent of infection locally and nationally, thus making it harder to plan an effective response for communities as well as individuals.

On the civil and political side, conflict situations, breakdown of law and order, poor legal frameworks and enforcement mechanisms, together with the denial of organizational rights and collective bargaining, hamper development in general and undermine essential health promotion measures in particular. In many countries, poorly resourced health systems, already weakened by debt and structural adjustment, have been unable to provide the care or the prevention needed.

In summary, a climate of discrimination and lack of respect for human rights leaves workers more vulnerable to infection and less able to cope with AIDS because it makes it difficult for them to seek voluntary testing, counselling, treatment or support; they will also not be in a position to take part in advocacy and prevention campaigns.

Factors that increase the risk of infection for certain groups of workers

Certain types of work situations are more susceptible to the risk of infection than others although the main issue is one of behaviour, not occupation. The following is an indicative list:

- work involving mobility, in particular the obligation to travel regularly and live away from spouses and partners;
- work in geographically isolated environments with limited social interaction and limited health facilities;
- single-sex working and living arrangements among men;
- situations where the worker cannot control protection against infection;
- work that is dominated by men, where women are in a small minority;
- work involving occupational risks such as contact with human blood, blood products and other body fluids, needle-stick injury and infected blood exposure, where Universal Precautions are not followed and/or equipment is inadequate.

To this list could be added "non-work", in order to cover situations where: unemployed workers, congregating in urban centres in the hope of obtaining any kind of small income, are exposed to HIV-susceptible pressures, or displaced persons and refugee camp inhabitants, likewise unoccupied and feeling abandoned, may turn to sex or be forced into it, especially the many single mothers in such situations.

The special needs of the informal sector[1]

Informal workers are especially likely to suffer from the consequences of AIDS, first, because they cannot usually access health facilities or social protection benefits available to workers in formal employment; second, because their activities are rarely based on or lead to financial security; and third, because the transient and vulnerable nature of their work means that any absence will probably result in the loss of the means of trading or production. For informal businesses, the loss of one or more employees may have major consequences leading to the collapse of the enterprise. If the owner contracts HIV, becomes ill and dies, the diversion of the enterprise's capital into treatment, care and funeral costs may ruin future reinvestment, cause bankruptcy, and leave dependent employees and family members bereft. In the rural informal sector, the burden of care often results in the diversion of labour away from agricultural activities, while labour losses due to AIDS lead to lower food production and declining longer term food security. Overall, the downward

---

[1] According to the ILO Director-General's Report to the International Labour Conference in 1991, the term "informal sector" [is] understood to refer to very small-scale units producing and distributing goods and services, and consisting largely of independent, self-employed producers in urban areas of developing countries, some of whom also employ family labour and/or a few hired workers or apprentices; which operate with very little capital, or none at all; which use a low level of technology and skills; which therefore operate at a low level of productivity; and which generally provide very low and irregular incomes and highly unstable employment to those who work in it. They are informal in the sense that they are for the most part unregistered and unrecorded in official statistics; they tend to have little or no access to organized markets, to credit institutions, to formal education and training institutions, or to many public services and amenities; they are not recognized, supported or regulated by the government; they are often compelled by circumstances to operate outside the framework of the law, and even where they are registered and respect certain aspects of the law they are almost invariably beyond the pale of social protection, labour legislation and protective measures at the workplace. Informal sector producers and workers are generally unorganized (although informal local associations of those engaged in specific activities may exist), and in most cases beyond the scope of action of trade unions and employers' organizations (see ILC: *The dilemma of the informal sector*, 78th Session (1991), Report I(1), p. 4 (English text)).

economic spiral is felt particularly hard by informal businesses when the following pattern emerges: markets contract as consumers die or retain minimal disposable income because of the costs of health treatment and care.

The gender dimension

HIV/AIDS affects women and men differently in terms of vulnerability and impact. There are biological factors which make women more vulnerable to infection than men, and structural inequalities in the status of women that make it harder for them to take measures to prevent infection, and also intensify the impact of AIDS on them.

– Many women experience sexual and economic subordination in their marriages or relationships, and are therefore unable to negotiate safe sex or refuse unsafe sex.

– The power imbalance in the workplace exposes women to the threat of sexual harassment.

– Poverty is a noted contributing factor to AIDS vulnerability and women make up the majority of the world's poor; in poverty crises, it is more likely to be a girl child who is taken out of school or sold into forced labour or sex work.

– Women's access to prevention messages is hampered by illiteracy, a state affecting more women than men worldwide – twice as many in some countries.

– Women make up a substantial proportion of migrants within countries and, together with children, they represent over three-quarters of refugees; both of these states are associated with higher than average risks of HIV infection. In conflict situations there is an increasing incidence of the systematic rape of women by warring factions.

– The burden of caring for HIV-infected family and community members falls more often on women and girls, thus increasing workloads and diminishing income-generating and schooling possibilities.

44

- Sexist property, inheritance, custody and support laws mean that women living with HIV/AIDS, who have lost partners or who have been abandoned because they are HIV positive, are deprived of financial security and economic opportunities; this may, in turn, force them into "survival sex"; the girl child is especially vulnerable to commercial sexual exploitation.

- Studies show the heightened vulnerability of women, compared to men, to the social stigma and ostracism associated with AIDS, particularly in rural settings, thus leaving them shunned and marginalized; this again increases the pressure on them to survive through sex.

- The work that women carry out – paid or unrecognized – is more easily disrupted by AIDS: for example, women dominate the informal sector where jobs are covered neither by social security nor by any occupational health benefits.

- Fewer women than men are covered by social security or occupation-related health benefits.

- Men are often victims of stereotypes and norms about masculine behaviour which may lead to unsafe sex and/or non-consensual sex.

- Men are over-represented in a number of categories of vulnerable workers, and may also find themselves through their employment in situations which expose them to unsafe sex between men.

- Given the prevailing power relations between men and women, men have an important role to play in adopting and encouraging responsible attitudes to HIV/AIDS prevention and coping mechanisms.

Appendix II

Infection control in the workplace

A. Universal blood and body-fluid precautions

Universal blood and body-fluid precautions (known as "Universal Precautions" or "Standard Precautions") were originally devised by the United States Centers for Disease Control and Prevention (CDC) in 1985, largely due to the HIV/AIDS epidemic and an urgent need for new strategies to protect hospital personnel from blood-borne infections. The new approach placed emphasis for the first time on applying blood and body-fluid precautions universally to all persons regardless of their presumed infectious status.

Universal Precautions are a simple standard of infection control practice to be used in the care of all patients at all times to minimize the risk of blood-borne pathogens. Universal Precautions consist of:

- careful handling and disposal of sharps (needles or other sharp objects);
- hand-washing before and after a procedure;
- use of protective barriers – such as gloves, gowns, masks – for direct contact with blood and other body fluids;
- safe disposal of waste contaminated with body fluids and blood;
- proper disinfection of instruments and other contaminated equipment; and
- proper handling of soiled linen.

B. Selected guidelines and Universal Precautions on infection control

Bednarsh, H.S.; Eklund, K.J.: "Infection control: Universal Precautions reconsidered", in *American Dental Hygienists' Association: Access* (Chicago, 1995) Vol. 11, No. 1.

Centers for Disease Control and Prevention (CDC)/National Center for HIV, STD and TB Prevention/Division of HIV/AIDS Prevention:

Preventing occupational HIV transmission to health care workers (updated June, 1999).

South African Law Commission: *Aspects of the law relating to AIDS* (Project No. 85): Universal workplace infection control measures (Universal Precautions) (1997).

WHO: *WHO guidelines on AIDS and first aid in the workplace*, WHO AIDS series 7 (Geneva, 1990).

WHO/UNAIDS/ICN (International Council of Nurses): *HIV and the workplace and Universal Precautions*, Fact sheets on HIV/AIDS for nurses and midwives (Geneva, 2000).

Appendix III

A checklist for planning and implementing a workplace policy on HIV/AIDS

Employers, workers and their organizations should cooperate in a positive, caring manner to develop a policy on HIV/AIDS that responds to, and balances the needs of, employers and workers. Backed by commitment at the highest level, the policy should offer an example to the community in general of how to manage HIV/AIDS. The core elements of this policy, developed in sections 6–9 of this code, include information about HIV/AIDS and how it is transmitted; educational measures to enhance understanding of personal risk and promote enabling strategies; practical prevention measures which encourage and support behavioural change; measures for the care and support of affected workers, whether it is they or a family member who is living with HIV/AIDS; and the principle of zero tolerance for any form of stigmatization or discrimination at the workplace.

The following steps may be used as a checklist for developing a policy and programme:

- HIV/AIDS committee is set up with representatives of top management, supervisors, workers, trade unions, human resources department, training department, industrial relations unit, occupational health unit, health and safety committee, and persons living with AIDS, if they agree;
- committee decides its terms of reference and decision-making powers and responsibilities;
- review of national laws and their implications for the enterprise;
- committee assesses the impact of the HIV epidemic on the workplace and the needs of workers infected and affected by HIV/AIDS by carrying out a confidential baseline study;
- committee establishes what health and information services are already available – both at the workplace and in the local community;

- committee formulates a draft policy; draft circulated for comment then revised and adopted;
- committee draws up a budget, seeking funds from outside the enterprise if necessary and identifies existing resources in the local community;
- committee establishes plan of action, with timetable and lines of responsibility, to implement policy;
- policy and plan of action are widely disseminated through, for example, notice boards, mailings, pay slip inserts, special meetings, induction courses, training sessions;
- committee monitors the impact of the policy;
- committee regularly reviews the policy in the light of internal monitoring and external information about the virus and its workplace implications.

Every step described above should be integrated into a comprehensive enterprise policy that is planned, implemented and monitored in a sustained and ongoing manner.

Appendix IV

ILO documents

A. Resolutions, conferences, meetings and reports

Hodges-Aeberhard, J.: *Policy and legal issues relating to HIV/AIDS and the world of work* (ILO, Geneva, 1999).

—. *An outline of recent developments concerning equality issues in employment for labour court judges and assessors* (ILO, Geneva, 1997), see "Specific developments concerning HIV/AIDS discrimination", pp. 27-31.

ILO: *The role of the organized sector in reproductive health and AIDS prevention*, Report of a tripartite workshop for Anglophone Africa held in Kampala, Uganda, 29 Nov.-1 Dec. 1994 (Geneva, 1995).

—. *Report of the Meeting of Experts on Workers' Health Surveillance*, 2-9 Sep. 1997, doc. GB.270/6 (Geneva, 1998).

—. *Decent work*, Report of the Director-General, International Labour Conference, 87th Session, Geneva, 1999.

—. *Action against HIV/AIDS in Africa: An initiative in the context of the world of work*, based on the Proceedings of the African Regional Tripartite Workshop on Strategies to Tackle the Social and Labour Implications of HIV/AIDS, Windhoek, Namibia, 11-13 Oct. 1999 (Geneva, 1999).

—. *Resolution concerning HIV/AIDS and the world of work*, International Labour Conference, 88th Session, Geneva, 2000.

—. *Special High-Level Meeting on HIV/AIDS and the World of Work,* Summary of Proceedings of the Tripartite Technical Panel, Geneva, 8 June 2000.

—. *SIDA et milieu de travail: collecte de données au Togo* (Lomé, Sep. 2000).

—. *The extent and impact of the HIV/AIDS pandemic and its implications for the world of work in Tanzania*, Resource paper for ILO mission to the United Republic of Tanzania (Dar es Salaam, Sep. 2000).

—. *Conclusions and recommendations of the ILO pre-forum tripartite event on HIV/AIDS and the world of work*, African Development Forum 2000, Addis Ababa, Dec. 2000.

—. *Platform for action on HIV/AIDS in the context of the world of work: Panel discussion*, Report and conclusions of the Ninth African Regional Meeting (Abidjan, 8-11 Dec. 1999), Governing Body, 277th Session, Geneva, 2000.

—. *HIV/AIDS: A threat to decent work, productivity and development*, Document for discussion at the Special High-Level Meeting on HIV/AIDS and the World of Work (Geneva, 2000).

—. *HIV/AIDS in Africa: The impact on the world of work* (Geneva, 2000).

ILO/Ministry of Labour and Youth Development, United Republic of Tanzania: *Report for the national tripartite seminar for chief executives on strengthening workplace management in tackling employment implications of STI/HIV/AIDS* (Dar es Salaam, 2000).

N'Daba, L.; Hodges-Aeberhard, J.: *HIV/AIDS and employment* (ILO, Geneva, 1998).

Report on OATUU/UNAIDS/ILO Seminar on Trade Union Action against HIV/AIDS in Africa, Accra, 26-28 July, 2000.

B. Relevant ILO Conventions, Recommendations, codes of practice and guidelines

Discrimination (Employment and Occupation) Convention, 1958 (No. 111).

Vocational Rehabilitation and Employment (Disabled Persons) Convention, 1983 (No. 159).

Termination of Employment Convention, 1982 (No. 158), and Recommendation (No. 166).

Right to Organise and Collective Bargaining Convention, 1949 (No. 98).

Collective Bargaining Convention, 1981 (No. 154).

Occupational Safety and Health Convention, 1981 (No. 155), and Recommendation (No. 164).

Occupational Health Services Convention, 1985 (No. 161), and Recommendation (No. 171).

Employment Injury Benefits Convention, 1964 (No. 121).

Social Security (Minimum Standards) Convention, 1952 (No. 102).

Nursing Personnel Convention, 1977 (No. 149).

Migration for Employment Convention (Revised), 1949 (No. 97).

Migrant Workers (Supplementary Provisions) Convention, 1975 (No. 143).

Part-Time Work Convention, 1994 (No. 175).

Worst Forms of Child Labour Convention, 1999 (No. 182), and Recommendation (No. 190).

Management of alcohol and drug-related issues in the workplace: An ILO code of practice (Geneva, 1996).

Protection of workers' personal data: An ILO code of practice (Geneva, 1997).

ILO: *Technical and ethical guidelines for workers' health surveillance*, Occupational Safety and Health Series No. 72 (Geneva, 1998).

Code of practice on managing disability in the workplace (forthcoming).

Appendix V

International and national guidelines on HIV/AIDS

A. International

Council of Europe, European Health Committee: *Medical examinations preceding employment and/or private insurance: A proposal for European guidelines* (Strasbourg, May 2000).

Family Health International: *Private sector AIDS policy, businesses managing HIV/AIDS: A guide for managers* (Research Triangle Park, NC, 1999).

Office of the High Commissioner for Human Rights (OHCHR)/ UNAIDS: *HIV/AIDS and human rights: International guidelines* (New York and Geneva, 1998).

Southern African Development Community (SADC): *Code on HIV/ AIDS and employment in the Southern African Development Community* (Zambia, 1997).

UNAIDS: *Guidelines for studies of the social and economic impact of HIV/AIDS* (Geneva, 2000).

UNAIDS: *AIDS and HIV infection, information for United Nations employees and their families* (Geneva, 1999).

UNAIDS/IPU (Inter-Parliamentary Union): *Handbook for legislators on HIV/AIDS, law and human rights* (Geneva, 1999), see "Annotated international guidelines".

United Nations: Resolution 54/283 on the review of the problem of human immunodeficiency virus/acquired immunodeficiency syndrome in all its aspects, adopted by the General Assembly at its 54th Session, New York, 14 Sep. 2000.

United Nations Commission on Human Rights: *Discrimination against HIV-infected people or people with AIDS*, Final report submitted by Mr. Varela Quiros (Geneva, 28 July 1992).

WHO: *Guidelines on AIDS and first aid in the workplace*, WHO AIDS Series 7 (Geneva, 1990).

WHO/ILO: *Statement from the Consultation on AIDS and the workplace* (Geneva, 27-29 June 1988).

B. National

Government

Centers for Disease Control and Prevention: "1999 USPHS/IDSA Guidelines for the prevention of opportunistic infections in persons infected with human immunodeficiency virus", in *Morbidity and Mortality Weekly Report (MMWR)* (Atlanta), see Appendix: "Environmental and occupational exposures", 20 Aug. 1999, Vol. 48, No. RR-10, pp. 62-64.

Citizens' Commission on AIDS: *Responding to AIDS: Ten principles for the workplace* (New York and Northern New Jersey, 1988).

Minister of Public Service, Labour and Social Welfare, Zimbabwe: *Labour relations (HIV and AIDS) regulations* (Zimbabwe, 1998).

Namibian Ministry of Labour: *Guidelines for implementation of national code on HIV/AIDS in employment* (Namibia, 1998), No. 78.

Namibian Ministry of Labour: *Code of good practice: Key aspects of HIV/AIDS and employment* (Namibia, 2000), No. R. 1298.

South African Department of Health/Community Agency for Social Enquiry (CASE): *Guidelines for developing a workplace policy programme on HIV/AIDS and STDs* (Mar. 1997).

United States Department of Health and Human Services: *Small-business guidelines: How AIDS can affect your business* (Washington, DC, undated).

Western Australia Commission: *Code of practice on the management of HIV/AIDS and hepatitis at workplaces* (West Perth, Sep. 2000).

Employers' organizations

Caribbean Employers' Confederation: *A wake up call to employers in the Caribbean*, Presentations from the Conference on HIV/AIDS/STDs in the Workplace (Suriname, Apr. 1997).

Christie, A.: *Working with AIDS: A guide for businesses and business people* (Bradford and San Francisco, Employers' Advisory Service on AIDS & HIV, 1995).

Federation of Kenya Employers (FKE): *Code of conduct on HIV/AIDS in the workplace* (Kenya, 2000).

Loewenson, R. (ed.): *Company level interventions on HIV/AIDS – 1. What can companies do?* (Harare, Organization of African Trade Union Unity, 1997).

South African Motor Corporation (Pty.) Ltd.: *SAMCOR Policy/Letter on HIV/AIDS* (1999).

UNAIDS/The Global Business Council on HIV & AIDS/The Prince of Wales Business Leaders Forum (PWBLF): *The business response to HIV/AIDS: Impact and lessons learned* (Geneva and London, 2000).

UNAIDS: *PHILACOR Corporation: Private sector HIV/AIDS response (Philippines)*, Best Practice Collection (Geneva, 1999).

United States Office of Personnel Management: *HIV/AIDS policy guidelines* (Washington, DC, 1995).

Workers' organizations

American Federation of Labor and Congress of Industrial Organizations (AFL-CIO): *Resolutions on HIV/ AIDS* (1991 and 1993).

Canadian Labour Congress: *National policy statement on AIDS and the workplace. A guide for unions and union members* (Ottawa, 1990).

Caribbean Congress of Labour: *Role of trade unions in AIDS awareness, objectives and strategies*, Statement from Caribbean seminar on trade unions and HIV/AIDS, Sep. 1990.

International Confederation of Free Trade Unions (ICFTU): *Congress statement on fighting HIV/AIDS* (Revised) (doc. 17GA/8.14, 1 Apr. 2000).

ICFTU/Botswana Federation of Trade Unions: *The Gaborone trade union declaration on involving workers in fighting HIV/AIDS in the workplace* (Gaborone, Sep. 2000).

National Amalgamated Local and Central Government and Parastatal Manual Workers' Union (NALCGPMWU), Botswana: *Policy and workplace guidelines* (undated).

Service Employees International Union: *Fighting AIDS discrimination through union action* (Washington, DC, 1996).

Appendix VI

Sectoral codes, guidelines and information

Agriculture

Barnett, T.: "Subsistence agriculture", in Barnett, A.; Blas, E.; White-side, A. (eds.): *AIDS brief for sectoral planners and managers* (Geneva, GPA/UNAIDS, 1996).

du Guerny, J.: *AIDS and agriculture in Africa: Can agricultural policy make a difference?*, FAO Sustainable Development Department (Rome, 1999).

Schapink, D. et al.: *Strategy to involve rural workers in the fight against HIV/AIDS through community mobilisation programs, draft for review*, Paper discussed at a regional workshop on community participation and HIV/AIDS, June 2000, United Republic of Tanzania (Washington, DC, World Bank Rural HIV/AIDS Initiatives, 2000).

Southern Africa AIDS Information Dissemination Service (SAF-AIDS): *AIDS and African smallholder agriculture* (Zimbabwe, 1999).

Education

Education International: *AIDS: Save the children and teachers*, Executive Board resolution on HIV/AIDS and education (Brussels, 2000).

Florida International University (FIU) Health Care and Wellness Center/FIU AIDS Committee: *Action guidelines for FIU employees, HIV/AIDS information* (Florida, 1999).

FIU Health Care and Wellness Center et al.: *Action guidelines for students, HIV/AIDS information* (Florida, 1999).

Kelly, M.J.: "What HIV/AIDS can do to education, and what education can do to HIV/AIDS" (Lusaka, 1999), in *Best Practice Digest*, UNAIDS website.

Sexuality Information and Education Council of the United States (SIECUS): "HIV/AIDS peer education: New York City schools", in *SHOP Talk (School Health Opportunities and Progress) Bulletin* (Brooklyn), 16 Aug. 1996, Vol. 1, Issue 5.

UNAIDS: *School health education to prevent AIDS and STD: A resource package for curriculum planners* (Geneva, 1999).

University of Queensland: "HIV policy and guidelines", in *Handbook of university policies and procedures* (Brisbane, 2000).

World Consultation of Teachers' International Organizations: *Consensus statement on AIDS in schools* (undated).

Health

Centers for Disease Control and Prevention: "Recommendations for prevention of HIV transmission in health-care settings", in *Morbidity and Mortality Weekly Report (MMWR)* (Atlanta), 21 Aug. 1987, Vol. 36, No. 2.

Centers for Disease Control and Prevention: "Guidelines for prevention of transmission of human immunodeficiency virus and hepatitis B virus to health-care and public safety workers", in *Morbidity and Mortality Weekly Report (MMWR)* (Atlanta), 23 June 1989, Vol. 38, No. 5-6.

Centers for Disease Control and Prevention: "Public health service guidelines for the management of health care worker exposures to HIV and recommendations for post-exposure prophylaxis", in *Morbidity and Mortality Recommendations and Reports* (Atlanta, 1998), Vol. 47, No. RR-7.

Garner, J.S.: *Guidelines for isolation precautions in hospitals*, Hospital Infection Control Practices Advisory Control Committee, CDC (Atlanta, 1996).

ICN (International Council of Nurses): *Reducing the impact of HIV/AIDS on nursing-midwifery personnel* (Geneva, 1996).

United States Agency for International Development (USAID): *AIDS briefs, health sector* (Washington, DC, undated).

WHO/ILO: *Statement from the Consultation on action to be taken after occupational exposure of health care workers to HIV* (Geneva, Oct. 1989).

Hotel, catering and tourism

Caribbean Epidemiology Centre (CAREC): *HIV/AIDS in the workplace – A programme for the tourism industry*, Caribbean Tourism Health, Safety and Resource Conservation Project (CTHSRCP) (Trinidad and Tobago, 2000).

Evans, C.: *Private clubs and HIV/AIDS: A guide to help private clubs cope with the effects of HIV and AIDS*, Premier Club Services Department, Club Managers' Association of America (Alexandria, undated).

International Hotel and Restaurant Association/Pacific Asia Travel Association/UNAIDS: *The challenge of HIV/AIDS in the workplace: A guide for the hospitality industry* (Geneva and Paris, 1999).

Moomaw, P.: "When an employee says, 'Boss, I have AIDS'", in *Restaurants USA* (National Restaurant Association, Washington, DC), Mar. 1996.

United States Agency for International Development (USAID): *AIDS briefs, tourism sector* (Washington, DC, undated).

WHO: *Report of the Consultation on international travel and HIV infection* (Geneva, Mar. 1987).

WHO: *Statement on screening of international travellers for infection with human immunodeficiency virus* (Geneva, 1988).

Maritime and transport

Aerospace Medical Association Human Factors Committee (AsHFC): *Neurobehavioural testing of HIV infected aviators*, Draft position paper (Alexandria, 1996).

Bikaako-Kajura, W.: *AIDS and transport: The experience of Ugandan road and rail transport workers and their unions* (International Transport Workers' Federation, London, 2000).

International Transport Workers' Federation: *Proposals for a policy on HIV/AIDS prevention and care for transport workers in Uganda* (London, 2000).

Nueva Era en Salud/Civil Military Alliance to Combat HIV/AIDS: *The Panamanian International Maritime and Uniformed Services Sector STD/HIV/AIDS Project, executive summary* (1998).

Philippine Seamen's Assistance Program (PSAP)/ITF Seafarers' Trust: *PSAP AIDS education programme for Filipino seafarers* (Rotterdam, undated).

WHO/ILO: *Consensus statement from the Consultation on AIDS and seafarers* (Geneva, Oct. 1989).

Yeager, R.: *Inter-Organization Policy Meeting on the Development of HIV/AIDS Prevention in the Maritime Sector*, Background paper (London, Oct. 1997).

—; Norman, M.: "HIV and the maritime – Seafarers and seaport workers: A hidden population at risk", in *Civil-Military Alliance Newsletter* (Hanover, NH), Oct. 1997, Vol. 3, No. 4.

Mining and energy

Anglo American Corporation of South Africa Limited: *HIV/AIDS policy* (1993).

International Federation of Chemical, Energy, Mine and General Workers' Unions (ICEM), *Report and conclusions of workshop on HIV/AIDS* (Johannesburg, 2001).

United States Agency for International Development (USAID): *AIDS briefs, mining sector* (Washington, DC, undated).

World Bank/International Finance Corporation (IFC): *HIV/AIDS and mining*, IFC website.

Public service and military

Civil-Military Alliance (CMA)/UNAIDS: *Winning the war against HIV and AIDS: A handbook on planning, monitoring and evaluation of HIV prevention and care programmes in the uniformed services* (Geneva, 1999).

Vancouver Health Department: *AIDS in the workplace, education program for civic employees* (Vancouver, 1990).

Public Services International: *Policy and programme on HIV/AIDS for PSI affiliates and public sector workers* (Ferney-Voltaire, 2000).

UNAIDS: *AIDS and the military, UNAIDS point of view*, UNAIDS Best Practice Collection (Geneva, 1998).

United Nations Military Planners and Commanders/United Nations Department of Peacekeeping Operations and Civil Military Alliance to Combat HIV/AIDS: *Policy guidelines on HIV/AIDS prevention and control for United Nations military planners and commanders* (Geneva, Feb. 2000).

United States Agency for International Development (USAID): *AIDS briefs, military populations* (Washington, DC, undated).

Appendix VII

Selected educational and training materials and other information

American Federation of Government Employees: *An AFGE guide: Women and HIV/AIDS* (Washington, DC, undated).

American Federation of Labor and Congress of Industrial Organizations (AFL-CIO): *AIDS in the workplace: A steward's manual* (Washington, DC, undated).

American Federation of Labor and Congress of Industrial Organizations (AFL-CIO): *AIDS in the workplace: Labor's concern* (Washington, DC, undated).

American Federation of Teachers: *HIV/AIDS education project* (Washington, DC, undated).

Canadian AIDS Society/Canadian Union of Public Employees: *ACT NOW: Managing HIV/AIDS in the Canadian workplace – A policy development and education manual* (1990).

Canadian Union of Public Employees: *Information kit on HIV/AIDS and the workplace* (Ontario, 2000).

Communications Workers of America: *CWA and US West respond to AIDS* (1994).

Leather, S.: "Why AIDS is a trade union issue", in *Scientific World*, 1992, Vol. 36, No. 2.

National Union of Namibian Workers (NUNW): *HIV/AIDS basic training manual* (Namibia, 1995).

Rosskam, E.: *AIDS and the workplace,* one module of *Your health and safety at work: A modular training package* (ILO, Geneva, 1996).

Public Services International: *Focus* (Ferney-Voltaire), Vol. 8, No. 1.

Service Employees International Union: *AIDS education project* (undated).

Service Employees International Union: *HIV/AIDS book: Information for workers* (1991).

South African Motor Corporation (Pty.) Ltd.: *Handbook on HIV/AIDS* (2000).

The Building Trades Group of Unions Drug and Alcohol Committee: *AIDS: Get real, get safe* (Sydney, undated).

UNAIDS: *HIV/AIDS and the workplace: Forging innovative business responses*, UNAIDS Best Practice Collection (Geneva, 1998).

United Nations Department of Peacekeeping Operations: "Module 1: Defining HIV and its impact on the military", in *HIV prevention and behaviour change in international military populations* (New York, 1999).

Whiteside, A.; Sunter, C.: *AIDS: The challenge for South Africa* (Human & Rousseau, Cape Town and Tafelberg, 2000).